Ella Fitzgerald
American Jazz Singer

by Grace Hansen

Abdo
HISTORY MAKER
BIOGRAPHIES
Kids

abdopublishing.com

Published by Abdo Kids, a division of ABDO, PO Box 398166, Minneapolis, Minnesota 55439.

Copyright © 2016 by Abdo Consulting Group, Inc. International copyrights reserved in all countries.
No part of this book may be reproduced in any form without written permission from the publisher.

Printed in the United States of America, North Mankato, Minnesota.

102015

012016

Photo Credits: AP Images, Corbis, Getty Images, iStock, Library of Congress, Shutterstock,
©Carl Van Vechten p.5

Production Contributors: Teddy Borth, Jennie Forsberg, Grace Hansen

Design Contributors: Laura Mitchell, Dorothy Toth

Library of Congress Control Number: 2015941768

Cataloging-in-Publication Data

Hansen, Grace.

 Ella Fitzgerald: American jazz singer / Grace Hansen.

  p. cm. -- (History maker biographies)

Includes index.

ISBN 978-1-68080-124-8

1. Fitzgerald, Ella, 1917-1996--Juvenile literature. 2. Jazz musicians--United States--Biography--
Juvenile literature. 3. African American jazz musicians--Biography--Juvenile literature. 1. Title.

782/092--dc23

[B]

2015941768

Table of Contents

Birth & Early Life

Ella Fitzgerald was born on April 25, 1917. She was born in Newport News, Virginia.

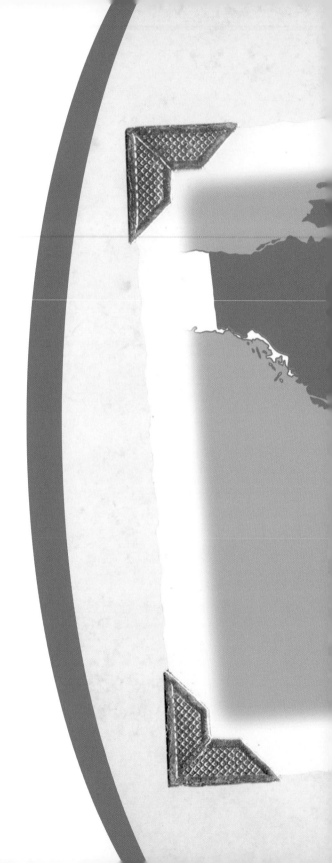

Virginia

Ella's family moved to Yonkers, New York. Ella's mother died in 1932. She moved in with her aunt.

The Apollo

By 1934, Ella was living on the streets. She entered a **contest** at Harlem's Apollo Theater. She hoped to win the prize money. She sang two songs.

9

The audience loved Ella. So, she entered many more **talent** shows. And she kept winning!

11

In 1935, Ella recorded her first song. It was called, "Love and Kisses." She was also performing at the Savoy. It was a **famous** ballroom.

13

Fame!

In 1938, Ella recorded "A-Tisket, A-Tasket." It was very popular. It sold 1 million copies! Ella was **famous**.

15

The 1950s and 1960s were great for Ella. She made very popular music. The very first Grammy Awards was held in 1958. Ella won two **Grammys**!

17

Ella went on to win 13 **Grammys**.

She recorded over 200 albums

and 2,000 songs! She won many

other awards. She also gave a

lot to **charity**.

19

Death & Legacy

On June 15, 1996, Ella died.

She was at her home in

Beverly Hills, California.

She is remembered as

"The First Lady of Song."

Timeline

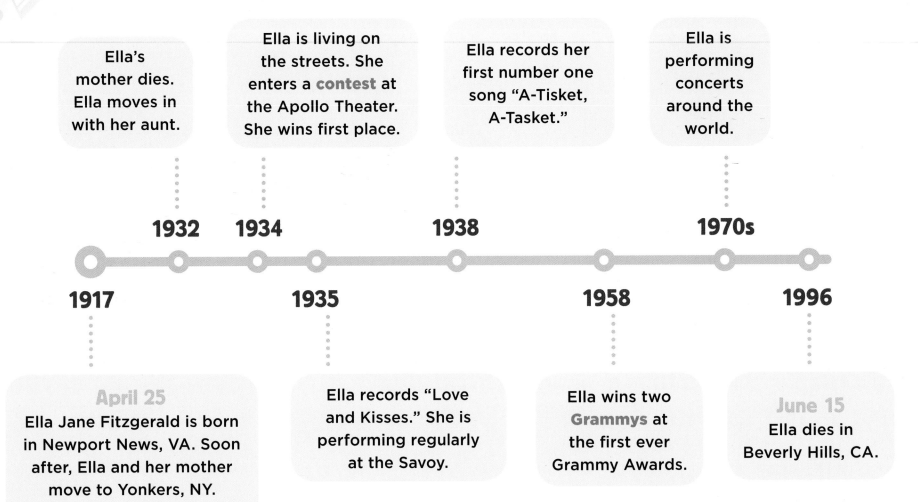

Ella's mother dies. Ella moves in with her aunt.

Ella is living on the streets. She enters a **contest** at the Apollo Theater. She wins first place.

Ella records her first number one song "A-Tisket, A-Tasket."

Ella is performing concerts around the world.

1932   **1934**   **1938**   **1970s**

1917   **1935**   **1958**   **1996**

April 25
Ella Jane Fitzgerald is born in Newport News, VA. Soon after, Ella and her mother move to Yonkers, NY.

Ella records "Love and Kisses." She is performing regularly at the Savoy.

Ella wins two **Grammys** at the first ever Grammy Awards.

June 15
Ella dies in Beverly Hills, CA.

Glossary

charity – generous donations and actions to aid the poor or ill.

contest – a competition for a prize.

famous – well-known by many people for something you do.

Grammy – a statue awarded by the National Academy of Recording Arts and Sciences for outstanding achievement.

talent – a unique and natural ability.

Index

abdokids.com

Use this code to log on to abdokids.com and access crafts, games, videos, and more!

Abdo Kids Code:
HEK1248